A Red Quilt

by Alex Quan
illustrated by C. A. Nobens

Practice Decodable 12

McGraw Hill Education

Bothell, WA • Chicago, IL • Columbus, OH • New York, NY

MHEonline.com

Send all inquiries to:
McGraw-Hill Education
8787 Orion Place
Columbus, OH 43240

ISBN: 978-0-02-144953-8
MHID: 0-02-144953-8

Printed in the United States of America.

7 8 9 CTM 23

What can Ben get?

Greg has red pens.
Peg has quilts.

Her quilts go on a bed.

Her quilts can go in a den.

What is best?

Ben gets a red quilt.

It has hens on it.